Just a S

Wendy Blaxland
illustrated by Caroline Magerl

Blaxland, Wendy, 1949–.
Just a seed.

ISBN 1 86388 609 5.

1. Readers (Primary). I. Magerl, Caroline.
II. Title. (Series: Reading discovery.)

428.6

First published in 1996 by Scholastic Australia Pty Limited ACN 000 614 577,
PO Box 579, Gosford 2250. Also in Sydney, Brisbane, Melbourne, Adelaide and Perth.

Printed in Hong Kong.

9 8 7 6 5 4 3 2 1   6 7 8 9 / 9

SCHOLASTIC
SYDNEY AUCKLAND NEW YORK TORONTO LONDON

'Just a seed,' said the girl,
and she threw it away.

'Just a seedling,' said the butterfly, and she sat on it.

'Just a sapling,' said the dog,
and she sniffed it.

'Just a tree,' said the bird,
and she nested in it.

'Just a flower,' said the artist, and she painted it.

'Just an apple,' said the boy,
and he picked it.

'Just a seed,' said his mother,
and she threw it away.